SHINGLED HOUSES
in the Summer Sun

The Work of Polhemus Savery DaSilva

by John R. DaSilva

Published in Australia in 2011 by

The Images Publishing Group Pty Ltd

ABN 89 059 734 431

6 Bastow Place, Mulgrave, Victoria 3170, Australia

Tel: +61 3 9561 5544 Fax: +61 3 9561 4860

books@imagespublishing.com

www.imagespublishing.com

National Library of Australia Cataloguing-in-Publication entry:

Author:	DaSilva, John R.
Title:	Shingled houses in the summer sun : the work of Polhemus Savery DaSilva / John DaSilva.
Edition:	1st ed.
ISBN:	9781864704372 (hbk.)
Subjects:	DaSilva, John R. Polhemus Savery DaSilva Architects Builders. Architecture, Domestic—Shingle style—United States. Architects—United States. Architectural firms—United States.

Dewey Number: 728.0973

Designed by John R. DaSilva in conjunction with Kendra Wallin and The Images Publishing Group. Set in Helvetica and Garamond.

Pre-publishing services by United Graphic Pte Ltd, Singapore

Printed on 140 gsm Gold East Matt paper by Everbest Printing Co. Ltd., in Hong Kong/China

IMAGES has included on its website a page for special notices in relation to this and our other publications. Please visit www.imagespublishing.com.

Front cover: The front of "Dune House," lit by the late afternoon sun. An approaching storm over Nantucket Sound (to the right of the house) emphasizes the dramatic sky.

Front dust jacket flap: The entry porch to "Cape Cod Cove" house is a screen wall of flattened, over-scaled columns and fan light.

Rear dust jacket flap: Another screen wall, this one of flattened "Gothic" details, encloses a screened-in porch on Martha's Vineyard.

Back cover: One of the porches at "Champlain's Bluff" faces both the rising and setting sun over harbor and outer beach beyond.

Page 1: A casual beach house is playfully "top-heavy" in a vaguely "Victorian" way.

Page 3: Invented columns frame salt pond, river, and distant ocean views. A simple deck provides a platform for enjoying it.

Page 4 and 5: The beachfront context at the back of the house shown on page 1. The "Victorian" high-game continues.

SHINGLED HOUSES
in the Summer Sun

The Work of Polhemus Savery DaSilva

John R. DaSilva
Foreword by Burton B. Staniar   Introduction by Peter Polhemus

images
Publishing

Contents

Opening Words: by Clients, Critics, Writers, Awards Juries

"The work of Polhemus Savery DaSilva beautifully melds the traditions of New England with the way we live today, affirming that an architecture of place trumps an architecture preoccupied with passing trends."

Robert A.M. Stern, architect; Dean, Yale School of Architecture

"It is a pleasure to work with a firm that is committed to excellence in design and construction but that also understands the importance of creating a good experience for its clients. PSD gave us a smooth process where budgets and schedules were agreed upon and met, and where clear communication was valued. Their experience was critical in handling tricky permitting and challenging site conditions. Their integrated design and construction process saved us from a lot of worry and showed us that our home could be everything we dreamed of and also be fun to create."

House at Little Beach client

"The quality, variety, and uniqueness of the projects … and the service they provide to their clients made PSDAB stand out … PSDAB has a great variety of architectural styles they command … and this was very impressive."

NAHB National Home Builder of the Year juror upon granting the prestigious award to PSDAB

"I always felt confident that the design concepts could be turned into reality because of the harmony that existed inside the firm … we were able to explore tangents freely and either embrace or discard them without tension."

Pepperwood client quoted in *Cape Cod & Islands Home*

" … they're livable works of art, fairly bursting with light … These homes capture an essence of summer that suits the Cape like beach glass along the shore."

Annie Graves, *Yankee Magazine*

" … successfully references Cape Cod vernacular, nineteenth-century Shingle Style and the fine designers of the English Arts and Crafts houses … The American and English precedents fit the character of its seaside location. The detailing and craftsmanship are excellent."

Bulfinch Awards jury on Champlain's Bluff

" … as playful as an afternoon at the beach, followed by a cookout … reflects a lack of formality in layout and with lightheartedness in details … We intend to be here … for a long, long time."

Popponesset client quoted in *The Boston Globe Magazine*

"The buildings of Polhemus Savery DaSilva feel like up-to-date evolutions of Cape Cod architecture, deeply influenced by shingle-style architecture. This connection … makes the designs of Polhemus Savery DaSilva natural to the place and at the same time feel fresh and of our time."

Cesar Pelli, architect and AIA Gold Medal winner, from his foreword to *Architecture of the Cape Cod Summer*

"Polhemus Savery DaSilva is a modern-day pioneer of the one-stop design-build practice, integrating architecture and construction approaches of the 'master builder' scenario."

Nancy Ruhling, *Period Homes*

"I love the idea of a dining room for larger gatherings and holidays. This one is just right—elegant but casual."

Oyster River client, quoted in *New England Home* magazine

"What PSD designed and built for us is a warm, open house with interesting architectural features that make efficient use of space while providing a whimsical feel that is both unique to the site and in keeping with local architectural themes."

Fog Hollow client

"The world of Polhemus Savery DaSilva is so enormously refreshing, as this work takes the best of the Cape's context together with the architect's own personal approach and melds them into a body of uncompromising domestic architecture."

Michael Graves, architect and Professor Emeritus, Princeton University

"Each house is a wish—a place of tranquility by the sea, where memories are made with families and friends … just the right setting for living out that particular vision of the endless summer."

Michael J. Crosbie, Ph.D., Chairman of the Architecture Department, University of Hartford, from the introduction to *Architecture of the Cape Cod Summer*

Foreword

I have been coming to Cape Cod, in the summer, for my entire life. I have owned or rented homes in a number of locations, but each was always lacking in one way or another. I am now very fortunate to have a house that suits me, and my wife Nancy, perfectly. It fits us when we want boisterous socializing or a quiet conversation; when we want to retreat into a novel or run around with our grandchildren; when we want to revel in the beauty of the landscape or when we need to clean the catch-of-the-day. Our classic modern furniture and antique pieces live happily within the clean lines of the house. Abstract paintings, Cape Cod landscapes, and whimsical African art are at home together here. It captures the light that is so special in New England, and expands the view that is so appreciated on the waterfront. It speaks of who we are and how we live. It has

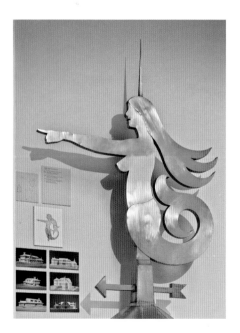

become a home for us, and our extended family, in the true sense of the word.

Given Nancy's background as an interior designer, and mine as an associate at Knoll, a leader in high-design furniture, we are well aware that achieving such a success takes a relationship, process, and attitude that clients and the professionals who work with them must share. For the creation of our home, Nancy and I were fortunate to find this in the partnership we had with Polhemus Savery DaSilva Architects Builders (PSD). They have a special approach that is quite unique in New England and served us very well. They aren't an architecture firm that also builds; nor are they a construction firm that also designs. They are committed to excellence in a fully integrated design–build scenario in which one does not dominate the other. They are at the top of both fields. I'm sure they would agree with me, however, that the fields should not be separated, as they are so often today, into the poorly related (and sometimes contentious) purveyors of creativity on one side and practicality on the other.

There are parallels between what PSD does to create great houses and what we do at Knoll to create classic furniture. We make furniture that often reaches the status of cultural icon and stays in demand, and production, for generations. For us, design and production must be different sides of the same coin—fully integrated with each other. No detail can be seen as too small for thoughtful consideration. Comfortable, long-lasting furniture integrates beauty and function. This integration starts with the very first

design ideas and continues through a carefully controlled process until the end user is satisfied. The process depends on strong relationships between team members—designers, engineers, suppliers, fabricators, sales people, administrators, and executives.

Beyond these parallels in process, there is also a strong relationship between successful physical results and how the businesses are run at both PSD and Knoll. While aesthetic sensibilities and craftsmanship skills are critical for success with both furniture and homes, for any design business to reach the top of its class it must also have a rigorous approach to organization, communication, and integrity. Quality in materials, fabrication, and design are critical but they are not enough. They have to be backed up by personal trustworthiness and accountability at every level of the organization. Service, honesty, teamwork, and fairness must be highly valued. Communication must be clear, consistent, and direct. Production sites must be orderly. Commitments must be honored. Accountability must be understood and welcomed.

When all of these things happen, the choreography of complexity that is the art and business of furniture making, architecture, and construction are made to seem effortless from the outside, even though they take hard work and careful planning on the inside. Beautiful furniture and homes, beloved by their users and recognized as timeless by the public, are the result.

For PSD, it seems that public recognition has indeed followed. Hardly a month passes when one of their projects isn't featured, or one of the principals isn't quoted, in print or on-line. In addition to the recognition inherent in the publication of both this book and their monograph, *Architecture of the Cape Cod Summer: The Work of Polhemus Savery DaSilva*, by a major international publisher, they are regular award winners. I congratulate PSD on receiving the National Association of Home Builders' 2010 National Custom Home Builder of the Year Award, a coveted and very competitive award. The Service Corps of Retired Executives recognized them in 2010 as the Cape Cod Business of the Year, and they have won numerous national, regional, and local design awards including one given for my house in the name and spirit of the great early American architect Charles Bulfinch. Through completing the process that created the house, and through living in it, I know first-hand how deserving PSD is of these honors.

Burton B. Staniar

Burton B. Staniar is Chairman of Knoll, Inc., a leading international design and furniture company. He was CEO of the company from 1993 until 2003. Prior to that, Burt was Chairman and CEO of Westinghouse Broadcasting and Cable, a leading multimedia company. He has also been an entrepreneur, and held a number of marketing and general management positions in companies such as Church & Dwight and Colgate–Palmolive. In addition, Burt serves on the board of a number of cultural and educational organizations.

Opposite: One of PSD's mermaids on display at Cape Cod Museum of Art (see page 11; 17, bottom; 29; 32, bottom right). Model photos and historical precedent for weathervane on wall beyond. Below: A classic shingle-style house sits on a private wind-swept site on Cape Cod. Its forms billow up as if ready to takeoff in the breeze, yet they stay held down by the columns. See page 22 for a closer view and page 34, bottom left, for the cupola to the right.

Introduction

A book on the work of one's own firm provides a summation of years of focus and hard work by many people. It showcases the results of our team's passion for design, construction, and client service. I also know that our clients share our passion, and that is deeply rewarding. Our vision of a process that integrates architecture and construction in a thoughtfully managed, carefully controlled manner results in beautiful, well-crafted homes.

Because of our success with this integration, we have been fortunate to win numerous design, construction, and business awards. We recently won the 2010 National Association of Home Builders' National Custom Home Builder of the Year Award. We are the first New England firm, and the first integrated architecture and construction firm anywhere, to achieve this. Our method has received further validation through imitation (the sincerest form of flattery!). When we established the firm in 1996 there were few comparable firms in New England. Some have since changed their way of working, and some new ones have evolved, to follow our integrated model. I believe these firms understand what we know—it is the best way to build custom homes today. The peace of mind, schedule control, budget control, and clear communications resulting from integrating design and construction serves our clients well. Usually they are busy people who live elsewhere when they begin the process of creating a home. They need a trustworthy, knowledgeable representative who can shepherd their project—from site selection through initial programming, design, permitting, construction, and ongoing maintenance—without the contentiousness that is often part of the construction process.

The regions in which we work are highly regulated. Most of our projects have at least one environmental, zoning, or historic regulatory hurdle, and often they have several. Negotiating the regulatory commissions takes skill and experience, both to achieve our client's goals and to protect the natural and built environment in which we work. Single-source responsibility gives these agencies confidence that we will do the right thing—that the environment won't suffer due to lack of communication or of accountability. This confidence provides great rewards for our clients.

The majority of the images in this book are from projects completed after *Architecture of the Cape Cod Summer: The Work of Polhemus Savery DaSilva* was published in 2008. We are fortunate to have had interesting projects for exceptional clients throughout these several years of challenging economic times. The honing of our business skills during this period has made us a stronger and more disciplined organization, even better able to provide value to our clients.

Peter Polhemus

Principals, Credits, Acknowledgments: Polhemus Savery DaSilva Architects Builders (www.psdab.com) is an integrated architecture and construction firm based in Chatham, MA, on Cape Cod. Its Principals are Architect and Builder **Peter Polhemus**, A.I.A., *President* and *CEO* (center), who attended Harvard, Goddard College, and MIT; Architect **John R. DaSilva**, A.I.A., *Design Principal* (left), who attended Princeton and Yale; and Builder **Aaron Polhemus**, *Chief Operating Officer* (right), who attended The University of Vermont. We thank our clients for making our work possible and deeply rewarding. Thanks to Kendra Wallin for the spectacular organization she brought to bear on the creation of this book; to Jeffery Brown, Aaron Udvardy, and Gerry Madden for preparing photographs and drawings to appear in it; to Sharon DaSilva, *Senior Designer*, for her partnership in formulating the ideas behind these buildings, for taking the lead on the design of some of them, and for proofreading the text; and to the rest of our staff for the care and commitment they show as well (Jerry Durr, *Architectural Operations Manager*; Perry Ermi, *Construction Operations Manager*; Richard Manfredi, *Chief Financial Officer*; Sean Mulcahy, *Senior Estimator*; Jon Carpenter, Fran Cattuti, Andrew Davol, Steve Glasheen, Deb Guay, Rick Lawrence, Bernie Linehan, Kiel Lombardozzi, Chris Maffei, Bryan McCorkle, Dennis Milan, Kevin Miller, Marcia Morse, Brett Nichols, Amanda Sawyer, Pete Schmeck, Melissa St.Onge, Nancy Swensson, Ray Tourville, and Jimmy Zinno). We thank the consultants and trade partners who share our values and commitments, including the landscape, interior, kitchen, and other designers whose work appears here (Richard Turlington, Taqua Glass, Architectural Glass Art, Donna Mahan, Tom Huckman, Hawk Design, Clara Batchelor, Phil Cheney, Paul Miskovsky, Abrahamson and Associates, Classic Kitchens and Interiors, Susan Tuttle, Kyle Timothy Blood, Herb Acevedo, Jody Trail, Suzanne Little, Nancy Staniar, Dorothy Eckman, Weena and Spook, Denise Maurer, and Irvine and Fleming) and the photographers whose work here represents our work so well (Brian Vanden Brink, Randall Perry, Dan Cutrona, Peter Aaron/ESTO, Paul Rocheleau, Greg Premru, Warren Jagger, G. Madden/PSD, and J. DaSilva/PSD). Last but not least, we thank our families (including Benjamin DaSilva Jr., who proofread the text) for their love and support.

Shingled Houses in the Summer Sun

-or-

Dream Homes Through Integrated Architecture and Construction

"You bind the goods and trappings of your life together with your dreams to make a place that is uniquely your own … The ordering of rooms can provide a context for daily action, and arranging the machines in an orderly way can ennoble specific acts. But still another realm of concern is necessary to make a good house. The dreams which accompany all human actions should be nurtured by the places in which people live."

Charles Moore, Gerald Allen, Donlyn Lyndon, *The Place of Houses*, 1974

Harriet Beecher Stowe, the 19th-century social reformer, first identified the single-family home as our country's great spiritual center. This is even more true in today's highly complex world than it was in Stowe's. On a personal level, for most people one's own home, along with the family that occupies it, is the spiritual center of one's life. As Moore et.al. so eloquently stated, our dreams are bound with, and nurtured by, our homes. For these reasons, creating a home is an important and challenging experience. This book is a small way to start thinking about that challenge. More than just a picture book, it is a catalog of dreams and possibilities for those considering their own shingled house in the summer sun. It highlights aesthetic and intellectual ideas embodied in forms and spaces, and the integration of thoughtful design and skillful craft that it took to execute those ideas.

As designers, we like contradictions and oxymorons, and the challenge of keeping them in balance. On the one hand, we can appreciate architecture as defined by Le Corbusier, the great 20th-century Swiss architect: "the learned game, correct and magnificent, of forms assembled in the light." On the other, we agree with Michael Graves, who defined architecture as a language with grammatical rules within which an infinite variety of combinations and inventions are possible. The houses we create should be fresh and of our time, yet they should also evoke the familiar and the timeless—they should be new and old at the same time. They should be unique and express the uniqueness of their occupants, but also be within established architectural vocabularies—a part of, rather than a break from, the continuum of architectural history. They should be

Below: A broad gambrel roof anchors a rambling shingle-style house on the waterfront. See page 17 & 29 for a rear view, and page 26 (top middle and top right) for the porch.

extraordinary in their spatial and expressive qualities but also skillfully crafted and comfortably connected to the ordinary and the everyday. They should be restrained and exuberant at the same time; elegant, but whimsical and fun.

In Vitruvius' *Ten Books* (Rome, circa 25 BC), the earliest surviving text on the subject, architecture and construction were balanced into the triumvirate of "firmness, commodity, and delight." The integration of durability, function, and beauty must be achieved such that they are indistinguishable as separate entities. Well designed buildings contribute beauty to their surroundings such that their presence—as well as their function, systems, and materials—are based on sustainability. Well designed buildings look composed, often with relationships of parts that seem obvious, even simple, although this takes great skill and complexity to achieve.

The process that achieves all this, however, should not involve contradiction at all. Architecture and construction, as both an art and a service to clients, are best served by a smooth and seamless method. Homes should be dream homes in the true sense of the term—personally suited to, expressive of, and inspirational to, the clients who occupy them. They must become the client's very own spiritual center; uniquely their own, as Moore et.al. suggest. The complexity of the steps necessary to

achieve this cannot be allowed to overwhelm the client. It must remain enjoyable and as satisfying as the end result.

The title of our previous book, a monograph called *Architecture of the Cape Cod Summer: The Work of Polhemus Savery DaSilva*, was a take on a book about the Shingle Style by Robert Stern and Vincent Scully called *The Architecture of the American Summer: The Flowering of the Shingle Style* (1989). Ours was a fitting title because the Shingle Style, the great American invention of casual, eclectic wooden homes wrapped in shingles, is a major influence on our work. The title of this companion volume is also a slight borrowing, this time from a pair of influential older books, *A Small House in the Sun* (1936) and *Cape Cod in the Sun* (1937), both by Samuel Chamberlin, the great photographer of New England. While Stern and Scully were focused on a high-style architectural movement, Chamberlin focused on vernacular architecture as highlighted by the crisp summer sun. This architecture is also a major source of inspiration for our work.

Vernacular building traditions are essentially design–build traditions in which the designer and builder work together, or are one and the same. The design and the production are of equal importance, and minimally distinguishable from each other. Unlike "signature" architecture of today, where buildings

Below: Details that are clever and precise indicate care and thoughtfulness in both design and execution. Here they are based on playful reinterpretations.

are designed to be more about an individual's artistic or intellectual ideas regardless of location, vernacular buildings grow out of local context, environmental response, users' needs and resources, and practical building methods. They employ tried and true forms and techniques developed over time to achieve durable, serviceable buildings fit to their purpose. They look right in whatever sun falls on them because they are in harmony with their locations. We try to learn from the vernacular—not just to emulate it but to transform it; to elevate it enough to be special but not so much as to be outrageous or avant-garde. This does not mean design ideas are of lesser importance. They are integral with, and do not come at the expense of, context, environment, functional need, budget, and constructability.

There is no room in vernacular architecture for the mentality of Howard Roark, the fictional architect in Ayn Rand's *The Fountainhead* whose individual creation must either triumph over all else, including the client's will, or be destroyed. While style and individual expression can and should play roles in any vernacular architecture, neither intransigent egotism nor quickly passing trends have a place. New forms or styles are tested by time before being absorbed. Of its own time but comfortable in any, vernacular design becomes timeless. It grows organically

and regionally. It can be associated with national movements, but they are always modified by local conditions. It can be eclectic rather than pure. How wonderful it is to see Greek and Gothic revival elements, for example, combined in mid-19th-century houses along Cape Cod's Old King's Highway.

With the publication of *Learning From Las Vegas* in 1972, architects were liberated to once again relate to the vernacular after a long period of often stale modernism. Controversial as it was, and still is, to take the architecture of the commercial sprawl of Las Vegas, learn from it and apply it, the authors (Venturi, Scott Brown and Izenour) teach us that we can learn from any vernacular, in any context. It is our goal to go one step further, to thoughtfully integrate vernacular and high-style design, without irony and not as a commentary on one or the other, but as an appropriate way to build homes that meet clients' needs, suit their environment, are responsible with respect to the sustainability of resources, and contribute to the art and craft of architecture and construction. Our goal is to succeed equally on all of these grounds and we have found that an integrated method, sometimes called design–build, is best for achieving this.

Integrated architecture and construction may today seem like an unusual method, but it is really an old idea. Through much

Below: A major exhibition at the Cape Cod Museum of Art shared its title with our previous book. PSD designed and built the museum and this gallery within it.

of history the concept of architect and general contractor as separate entities did not exist—siting and designing, drawing and model building, determining cost, organizing the labor, requisitioning materials, scheduling and directing the progress of the work, etc. were all the responsibility of one entity. In ancient Greece the term Architekton encompassed master carpenters and other building artisans. In the Middle Ages the notion of a building designer as separate from its constructors was almost non-existent—master masons and builders were also designers. One of the greatest building achievements of the Renaissance, the dome on the Florence Cathedral, was created under the Capomaestro system, where a master builder was the designer, director of the work, and, in this case, a brilliant problem solver who determined how to build what remains to this day the largest masonry dome in the world. It is telling that the Design Build Institute of America's highest award is named after Brunelleschi, the Capomaestro behind this accomplishment.

In colonial America, master artisans as well as gentlemen who designed as a pastime, like Thomas Jefferson, were considered architects. It wasn't until the 1820s that the disciplines of architecture and construction began to move

apart, and not until the late 19th century that building artisans and professional architects were commonly seen as separate entities. They have been diverging more and more ever since. This is not to the benefit of building owners and users, or to the benefit of the disciplines of architecture and construction.

In a very different time, place, and cultural context, the cottage Thoreau built for himself at Walden Pond was a vernacular design–build exercise. Thanks in part to Thoreau, the primitive hut as basic shelter is ingrained in the American psyche (although it has European origins as well). It is, of course, impractical to design and build one's house as Thoreau did (and actually for him it was really more a literary–philosophical exercise than a long-term solution to his shelter needs— he went home to mother's to do his laundry!). To build a great custom home today, and to enjoy doing it, takes an experienced, well-integrated team working together with the same values and toward the same goals.

The "Howard Roark" hero–architect, lording over a process where everything is subordinate to his genius, is the wrong model for today. The complexity of creating beautiful, well-crafted buildings that are sustainable on both technical and aesthetic grounds, requires collaboration in addition to aesthetic inspiration. It requires the skills, insights, and experience of many. With the right team working in the right way, creativity, craftsmanship, and sustainable practices are enhanced, not diminished. The streamlined process is most likely to improve value and to save time and hassle for the client—they don't have to assemble, manage, and referee a team since a highly functioning, pre-existing team is already available to them. With process and results improved, it is more fun for everyone involved, including, most importantly, the client.

Creating a new home, or renovating an old one, includes a high degree of emotional involvement. Most of our clients seek playful, comfortable places where they can take a deep breath and relax—they want a shingled house in the summer sun. They deserve a positive experience in achieving it. Through designing and building a house, clients are realizing a dream—sometimes one they have had throughout their entire lives. It can and should be an enjoyable experience for them, infused with a passion that is at least as strong on their part as it is on ours. A focused, well-managed, integrated architecture and construction method gives them the best chance of achieving this.

Integrating architectural design and construction is a logical idea that serves clients better than any other method available today for the creation of custom homes. It ensures that the

architect and builder, as a single source entity, are working harmoniously; a goal that seems obvious, but all too often fails to occur. Single-source responsibility and accountability for design, management, scheduling, estimating, constructing, cost guarantees, job site organization, communication, quality control, and a host of other critical activities, is difficult to master. When it is mastered, however, it has the potential to take frustration, stress, and time out of, and put value into, the experience for the client. When all team members come from within the same organization there is no finger pointing, no undermining of others, and no shifting blame.

Eventually, any thoughtful architect has to come to terms with a process of building, and any thoughtful builder has to come to terms with a process of designing. When architects learn to think like builders, and when builders learn to think like architects, the contribution each makes to the process of creating great homes is increased. The integration of art and craft, and the smooth operation that results, leads to the fulfillment of clients' dreams. Those dreams are represented here, on the pages of this book, and our hope is that they will inspire new dreams in everyone who looks at them.

Opposite: Every curve and every step is deliberate (see page 78, top right, for more of this fireplace).

Right: A central window located so the lighthouse is framed in the view (see page 45 for more of this space).

The Genius of Place: Working With Nature and the Sun

"Consult the genius of the place in all;
That tells the waters to rise, or fall;
Or helps th' ambitious hill the heav'ns to scale,
Or scoops in circling theatres the vale;
Calls in the country, catches opening glades,
Joins willing woods, and varies shades from shades,
Now breaks, or now directs, th'intending lines;
Paints as you plant, and, as you work, designs."

Alexander Pope, *Epistles to Several Persons*, 1732

Above: A woodland Gothic style helps marry the house to the natural context on this marshside site. Hardly a neighbor is visible, but the ocean is, beyond the marsh to the north.

Opposite: A gate mimics the forms of the house. The drive takes visitors up a small rise.

In his book *The Perfect House*, Witold Rybczynski pointed out how the great 16th-century architect Palladio designed villas that derived much of their impact from their sympathetic relationship to their surroundings. Palladianism, as an architectural style, was at its peak in England when Pope wrote the verse above. While Frank Lloyd Wright gets much credit for bringing the outdoors in, the agricultural flatlands, canals, and foothills of the Veneto, and the picturesque landscapes of 18th-century England, were integral to the effectiveness of both the interiors and exteriors of the great villas of these eras. Today, we too strive for such a connection.

Siting a house and establishing the relationship between built form and natural, between building layout and climate, and between new construction and existing built context, are among the most important responsibilities in the creative process. It is critical to combine excellent stewardship of the environment and the need for certain homes to be sited for maximum enjoyment of views and outdoor living. Houses and landscapes should feel natural together, complement one another in character and in function, tread lightly upon one another, belong to one another, collaborate with one another. There should be sensible relationships between buildings, and between buildings and other man-made features.

Sunlight is a major organizational factor in establishing a house that works well and feels right. It is important to site houses and to design their parts to both take advantage of and control the light as the sun moves through the sky. Each interior and exterior room must be located to receive natural light at the most appropriate time of day for its use.

We are fortunate to work in some of the most beautiful landscapes in the world. They are also very fragile and very regulated. Often there are coastal bank and wetland issues, including removal of invasive species and reclamation of damaged areas. Complex regulatory oversight is required for such work. An integrated team that includes civil engineers, landscape architects, and environmental consultants in addition to architects and builders is best suited to handling such regulations and the often lengthy permitting process that comes with them. A prerequisite for being on such a team is a commitment to both the sustainable treatment of that environment and the satisfaction of client needs.

A classic shingle-style house between wooded wetlands and Nantucket Sound. The shingles wrap the form as if it were a balloon. See page 5 for approach.

An elegant Cape approached via a winding drive through the woods and past the guest cottage that shares the house's roof shape (see page 35 & 100, bottom left).

New "cottages" and walkways at the Wequassett Resort create a village atmosphere, especially in the fog. Rustic and refined are in balance here.

"Dune House" is a beach house in the true sense, at the edge of south-facing dunes. An expanse of conservation beach and dunes lies to the east.

A rambling shingle-style house fills as much of its site as possible but leaves the coastal bank untouched. See page 88 for the pool tucked in to the right.

Welcoming Face, Public Voice, Sense of Order: The Front

"What people do for themselves using their bodies and faces, their gestures and their voices, those who build for them do using architectural forms."

John Onians, *Bearers of Meaning*, 1988

The front of a home is its place of introduction, arrival, and transition. It must be appropriate both from the perspective of a car on the street and a pedestrian approaching on foot. It might provide a first impression that is unusual or eccentric, but it should always be friendly and welcoming. It is like what a child produces when asked to draw a house—the most basic place where "home" is defined for each family.

The front façade is the place where a home can most eloquently speak to the public about its occupants—where the nature of the architecture can express the attitudes or lifestyle of, or those desired by, the owner. Onians wrote that a front façade "might tell you as much about the owner as would a face-to-face encounter with the man himself." It takes a careful understanding of the client's personality, values, and desires to shape a public image that reflects who they are and what they want to say to the world.

The public front also establishes a home's relationship to its neighborhood. The scale, roof and eave heights, set-backs from the street or property lines, window styles, materials, shapes, and architectural style are all important in relating to neighbors. Sometimes this takes the form of referencing, sometimes contrasting.

A sense of intentional order is important at the front. If the location of the front door is not obvious there should be strong clues within the architecture. Overall symmetry (every element that is present on one side of a center line is also present on the other), localized symmetry (the overall is not symmetrical but segments within it are), and balanced asymmetry (where no elements are symmetrical but they are carefully placed and proportioned to create balance) are classic design strategies for giving order to façades.

Architectural history plays its biggest role at the front of the house. People often wish to be associated with a particular historical architectural style that they feel represents them best or with which they are most comfortable. Often they do not even realize this and what they say needs to be interpreted and translated into constructed form.

Complicating the task is the coordination of the exterior, and the story it has to tell, with spaces behind the façade. Frequently, when views and/or privacy and outdoor living are to the rear, plans are arranged so service spaces (entry hall, powder room, pantry, mud room, laundry room, garage) are toward the front. This shelters the living spaces from the street, or more public portion of the property, but it has the danger of giving an under-animated presentation to the front. To get the front right takes good listening, thoughtful interpretation, and clever designing.

Left: A relaxed house, yet still inspired by traditional Greek Revival "bar and gable" house types in the neighborhood.

Opposite bottom: A playful bungalow on a lake combines the Gothic Revival with a lake-house bungalow form.

Set at road's end, this beach house is a relaxing retreat with a monumental presence.

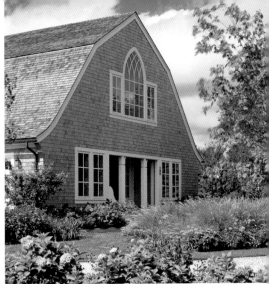

A friendly, welcoming gable and a big window.

A full two-story house is unusual in places where height limits are strict. The central skylight brings light into the entry space (see page 40, bottom right).

A story-book character is achieved through playful exaggeration.

A classic house with paired gables and a broad front porch.

Gridded windows set within weathered wood help create a classic shingle-style house. The driveway passes under the archway to the right.

Reminiscent of Adirondack cottages, N.E. mill buildings and Gothic Revival.

Vernacular N.E. seaside hotels were the inspiration (see page 60, bottom left).

Transition and Meaning: Entry, Porch, Screen Wall, Column

" ... to sit side by side, hand in hand,
in our chairs on the front porch of forever."

C.J. Heck, *Front Porch of Forever*, 2007

Porches mark entry and are the transition space between inside and out. They provide a place to linger before fully committing one's self to either. Like the entry hall on the other side of the door, front porches are a critical element in the sequences from public to private or, moving the other way, from private to public.

The front elevation conveys the major message of the house at the scale of the neighborhood. At the front entry the message of welcome must have clarity at a different scale—that of the human body. Information about the general nature of the home, such as "a formal place for big parties" or "an informal place for family fun" comes directly in contact with the visitor as they step onto the porch or reach for the door. This is the first intimate experience of the house and it should welcome and delight. It is often the most detailed place on the outside and it may be placed centrally in the composition. Sometimes other elements of the façade will inflect towards it or be subordinate to it.

Front porches as a place for sitting, holding hands, and watching the world go by get very little use in our era of air conditioning and virtual communities. Happy images of warm summer nights on the front porch are so culturally ingrained, however, that houses often don't feel right when they don't have one. Because of this symbolic importance, it is desirable to incorporate at least a "vestigial" front porch. Sometimes "porches" may be un-occupiable screen walls that function to break up sunlight and cast shadows—and as an expressive source of symbolic content. Sometimes the porch is like an arcade, intended for lateral passage across the front of the house from, for example, a parking area at one end to the front door in the center. When a full three-dimensional porch is not possible, but entry expression is still important, the porch and columns that define it can be compressed into pilasters in a flat door surround.

Porch roofs are often held up by columns. The repetition of columns and open bays in a porch can create pleasing rhythms that relate the structural function and scale of the building to the upright nature and scale of the human body. Columns bear more, however, than just weight. They are also "bearers of meaning," a phrase coined by historian John Onians to describe the symbolic function of the classical orders—columns and associated proportioning systems and rules of decorum. Architects of the Renaissance conferred status on clients by using classical columns on private villas. Previously they had been used primarily for public or religious buildings or for monumental palaces, and their meaning has changed over time. They have represented imperial might, Christian ascendancy, and personal values. They have projected a variety of moods, from sobriety to exuberance; of scales, from delicate to bold; of character, from refined to rustic. Symbolic associations have been many: mystical, spiritual, and religious; structural function; mathematical systems and music; the human body and gender; human emotion, morality, virtue, and dignity; social class; plant or animal forms—and this is just a partial list.

While strict use of the orders is only occasionally relevant to our work, the column as a symbolic bearer of meaning is very relevant, as is the importance of proportion at all levels of design. There is a difference between one-eighth of an inch and one-quarter of an inch—and this is critical for everyone involved in design and construction to understand. Because the details of porches, columns, and door surrounds are viewed from a close range, they are a place where design and construction skills are paramount.

Control of proportion and use of expressive architectural language that engages viewers was critical to orders-based architecture and it is critical to us, even when we are not using classical columns. Sometimes porches and screen walls are not created out of columns at all but out of walls that are perforated with shaped openings. Sometimes portions of the wall can be shaped to look like classical columns in frontal profile only. These become ambiguous elements that are both wall and column at the same time. This allows the porch or screen wall to carry its message playfully, evocatively, and without pure historical recreation. Columns, pilasters, and screen walls, and the front porches or door surrounds they establish, may be the architectural elements that throughout history have been the most subject to inventive change. We hope to continue this tradition, and to do so takes a concentration of creative energy and careful execution at this critical place in the home.

Opposite: A dramatic screen wall. See page 88, bottom right, for space beyond.

A variety of columns and piers from "correct" classical, to intentionally "incorrect" classical, to Gothic, to shingle-style. All have different and important stories to tell. Some are carpenter-crafted into playful reinterpretations of historical models, some are shingle or cedar board clad.

Above and below: Pineapples are a universal symbol of welcome, here made into flat pilaster capitols.

Leaf capitols and grooved boards clad structural posts.

Flat "cut-outs" for column, balastrade, and diamond shingles.

Joyful children as modern-day caryatids.

A shallow, but expressive, front porch.

Classical forms flattened into entry screen wall.

Flat columns transform into benches at bottom.

Children are everywhere—in the porch, the arched window, on top of the cupola, and inside at play at the Wequassett Resort Children's Center.

Backdrops for Rest & Play: Facing the Back Yard & the View

"I feel so very lucky
And I hold in great regard
The perfect little world
In my very own back yard!"

Marilyn Lott, *My Back Yard*, 2011

Back yards are typically activated by outdoor living much more than front yards. They are private space, akin to indoor space, that is available to a home's occupants but not usually to the public. The façade that faces the rear yard becomes a backdrop to a world-away. People are most likely to sit with their backs to it, facing the view or the landscape. Openings in the façade connect interior and exterior without need for the public-to-private transition space required at the front, although often a back porch provides an outdoor room that is both of the interior and of the exterior.

The scale and character of a back façade is often different from the front. It can be more expansive in relation to the expansiveness of a view or of a body of water. It may reveal an attitude about confronting the landscape rather than tucking in. Usually houses are located so the view, and the private space of the yard, are to the rear. To maximize views the house may be stretched across the property so as many rooms as possible participate. Ideally, houses are designed not just to take best advantage of the view, but to create the impression the view has been expanded.

Rear façades sometimes have bigger windows and fewer muntins (grids creating divided lights), giving them a different character. Windows may be grouped together into horizontal bands that make the interior rooms feel bigger and more connected to the outside. The overall feeling of the back may be more horizontal and flat, reflecting the window configuration and the rooms positioned across the plan to maximize view frontage; or it may be more vertical, stretching up to take advantage of more distant views. The back façade may have corner windows or projecting bays that expand views from straight out to panoramic and that bring in light from multiple exposures.

Right: The back yard slopes down to water's edge and is accessible from one corner of the deck through patio and planting space.

Opposite: A whimsical mermaid based on an historic weathervane in Maine presides over the fun (see page 6).

Outdoor living space behind grasses and trees (see page 12).

In contrast to the classic Cape front (page 33, bottom left), the back explodes up to upper-level spaces under a big roof and balconies facing the view.

"Dune House" has grass-covered dunes and Nantucket Sound as its yard.

The building whimsically peals up over the corner door (below).

The client wanted a wrap-around porch but footprint limitations allowed implied porch of pilasters only. The porch and interior living are compressed.

Here the view is perpendicular to the street so this "back" becomes an auto court, accessed through a porte cochere that is a "bridge" over the drive (see page 21).

The view from this house is equally strong in two directions. The master bedroom is to the left (see page 65), the living room to the right (see page 43).

Skyline Dance, Emphasis, Whimsy, Exaggeration: Exterior Details

"This preference of the genius to the parts is the secret … Art, in the artist, is proportion, or, a habitual respect to the whole by an eye loving beauty in details. And the wonder and charm of it is the sanity in insanity which it denotes. Proportion is almost impossible to human beings. There is no one who does not exaggerate."

R. W. Emerson, *Nominalist and Realist*, 1844

Scale plays a big role in the small parts that give character to a house. We like to exaggerate the size of exterior details like brackets, columns, and weathervanes. This makes them look both substantial and whimsical. Their exaggerated scale also brings the overall scale of the building down by confounding viewers' expectations of how big elements are in relation to each other. We like details that are flat on their faces but curvaceous in profile—taut and expressive of the crisp method of their making from one angle but gracious, even voluptuous, from another—simple in form but with big impact on scale and character.

Dormers announce that the roof is inhabited. They activate the roof and help make the house friendly. An extra small dormer can exaggerate the apparent size of the roof, emphasizing the primal nature of shelter. The symbolic impact of a roof is strengthened when repeated in miniature as a dormer. As the aedicule is a little building within, a dormer can be a little building upon the building. Dormers can create a regular cadence across a house or can dance up and down the roof in playful irregularity. Sometimes they emphasize a feature below by balancing horizontality and verticality. From the inside, a dormer is a cozy space to experience the impact of light, view, and the sheltering roof.

Cupolas, weathervanes, and finials provide a connection to the sky—a vertical emphasis that penetrates and points upward. As ornamental sign-boards they have an impact on the whole that is much greater than their small relative size. Along with dormers and chimneys, they add detail to a skyline that might otherwise be monotonous. Cupolas can also be critical for bringing in light.

Opposite: A projecting bay expands the view from inside (see page 2 & 45) and becomes a tower on the outside. A finial exaggerates the verticality of the tower.

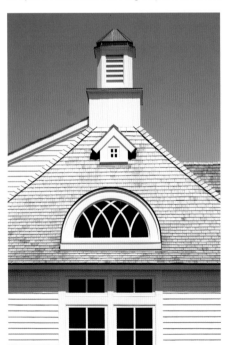

One dormer exaggerates the other.

Wooden chimney with flaring top mimics the trees.

Mini-screen wall and maxi-mermaid, pointing out to sea.

Ball and spike, above a special window.

The breeze has this volley lasting forever (see page 36, bottom left).

Drawing the eye to the sky and light into the space (see page 89, top).

Big fish on a classic cupola. It's the catch-of-the-day (see page 21, top).

The cupola brings in light while the golfing fool spins. Is it because of the martini or the wind?

The light-monitor floods the space below (see page 43, left). The mirror is so she can watch for unreliable seamen.

Profiles of actual children who posed to create a playful "sign" at the Wequassett Resort's Children's Center (see page 27, bottom).

Slight curves in the dormer gable gives a storybook feeling.

Looking through small dormer out to sea (see page 30, top left).

Small triangular dormers dance up a long slope clad with zinc-coated copper. The tiny windows have major impact on space within (see opposite, top left).

A big "W" is both sign and architectural bracket within an open eyebrow dormer.

A traditional fan light, or a spider's web? (see opposite, bottom left).

Dormers help shape the space with geometry and light (see page 41).

A dormer projecting onto the roof below can be a cozy bay window.

An interior balcony gives a view through the dormer out to the terrace.

See page 29 for external view of the dormer and page 3 for view from below.

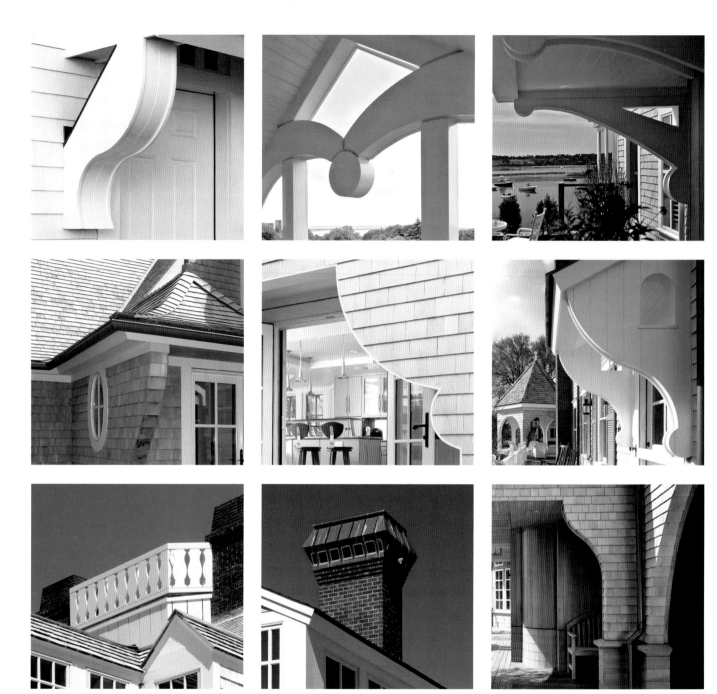

Above: Widow's walks, brackets, arches, and chimney caps are details where playful expression can be most exhuberant.

Opposite: Chunks of colored glass reflect the afternoon sun. The glass is embedded, along with pebbles, into mortar in a revival of the classic shingle-style "pebbledash" technique. The panel design mimics the colors of the sunset as seen from the back of the house (see page 14 and 28, top).

Choreographing Transition, Sequence & Drama: Entry Spaces

"The lavish attention that has been spent on entry places in all forms of architecture attests to the importance of territorial distinction between inside and out. The point of transition between the two has persistently been used as a spot where information is conveyed … "

Charles Moore et.al., *The Place of Houses*, 1974

Every home, no matter how small, should have an entry space distinct from its living space. A home feels imbalanced when there is no transition between public and private realms. If not left adequately behind, the public realm intrudes and the home fails to feel like a sanctuary. It is important that every home have a place where the ceremonies of arrival and departure can take place. This space prepares visitors for passage through the house. It is the first interior space in the sequence from public to private, and the first to be climate controlled. When it is placed and designed well, the house beyond unfolds naturally,

without feeling forced or overwrought. Whether it is large and formal or small and informal, it must be welcoming; an invitation to pause in pleasure before proceeding.

The entry provides orientation to guests. There is often a view from the entry through the house and out the back to the landscape or view beyond. In many homes, a stair is within, or adjacent to, the entry and this orients users vertically.

The entry hall Thomas Jefferson designed for himself at Monticello, one of America's most inventive classical houses, was intended to impress visitors with its high ceiling, abundant natural light, elaborate balcony, and museum-like displays. Awe-inspiring grandeur is sometimes still on the agenda for entry halls today, even when the rest of the house is casual. More modest entries are also popular. They may have direct connections to living space beyond. Here benches for putting on shoes, and closets for coats and other functional elements may be more visible.

A curved wall in the entry porch, along with a mahogony bench, directs visitors to the entry/stair hall that is off-center with the main gable (see page 9). The curved ceiling shape and pattern orients visitors to one of two hallways that radiate from it (see page 66, bottom left).

This more formal entry is on center and it leads to a grand hall (see page 42, top center), then to a vestibule where rooms radiate off in a "butterfly" plan (see page 67, top), and ultimately to the harbor beyond.

Right: A rich space acts as entry hall, stair, and gallery. Hints of Art Nouveaux, Bernard Maybeck's gothicism, and Piranesi's imaginary world—along with careful integration of structure, lighting, display space, and circulation flow—make for a complex but rewarding choreography. See page 79 for opposite perspective and page 63.

Below: The ceiling is low just inside the door.

New floor: looks like it was always there.

Baroque drama, bright light, and movement.

An historic door, once covered, now re-made and open to light.

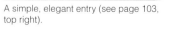

A simple, elegant entry (see page 103, top right).

Dynamic curves and grid of tiny windows.

A dramatic space defines entry but is also widely open.

Anti-clockwise from bottom center: Entry sequence
starts at "grotto" portal, moves up stair within
porch, through a mahogany door, and into tower
(see page 18).

Open Space for Relaxing Together: Family Rooms

A desire for freedom and relaxation was a big determinant of the shingle-style houses of the late 19th century. The casual lifestyles embodied in the architecture of these houses resonated with F. L. Wright. He perfected plans based more on a series of spaces than on a series of rooms and, for many, this is still desirable today.

Clients today rarely request formal living rooms. Most want space that promotes social interaction; where socializing, cooking, and dining are connected. As a result, the family room is often open to both kitchen and dining areas. To sustain the variety of activities that take place in them, and to nurture a variety of needs, houses should have a balance of open and closed spaces, and of communal and private spaces. A family room is weighted toward communal use, but might have a nook or window seat to allow simultaneous private use. Family rooms often include a seating area large enough for family and guests, smaller separate seating, fireplace, and television. Television versus fireplace is a tricky issue. Sometimes clients choose to have the television over the fireplace so both can be on center. Others choose to split-the-difference and put the center point between the television and fireplace. Others choose one or the other to dominate, or to have no television in the family space.

Usually the family room has the best view and light. The outlook this provides connects users to the world beyond. As in all major rooms, windows should occur on at least two sides. This is especially important where social interaction is frequent. There is less glare than if windows are only on one side; the portion of the day during which direct sunlight falls into the space is increased; and objects and people are lit more evenly, and are easier to look at and recognize. As the principal gathering space of the house, the family room should be highly inviting and draw people in; it should be a place to which they naturally gravitate. Since, as humans, we seem to instinctively move toward light, if the family room has the best light available it will be most likely to accomplish this.

Above and opposite: Dramatic space soars up and flows out to adjacent spaces that are both defined as separate from, and connected to, the main space.

An aedicula (building-within-a-building) defined by four cross-shaped columns. See page 42, bottom right, for the occulus that brings in light and page 85, bottom center, for columns

Whimsical brackets and archway loosely separate living and dining (see page 53).

A traditional living room at the "Moorings" restored to its historic former glory.

Opposite and above: Different attitudes about decorating, but all three of these living spaces focus on light and view, and all three have shapes in the ceiling.

Heartbeat and Nerve Center: Kitchens

A carved soapstone sink sits in a well-lit space with antique pine floors, three-dimensional tiles, and beautiful cabinetry.

The dining room is now partially open to the kitchen and family room.

" … more like the home's engine than its caboose."
Winifred Gallagher, *House Thinking*, 2006

The kitchen as the heart of the home has a long history in non-servant supported households. The kitchens of the earliest colonial homes of New England and farmhouses of the Midwest played this role, as do most today. There are few daily rituals of family life left, but the human need for regular meals keeps one alive, even when meal preparation is pared down to warming in the microwave. The kitchen is the place in typical homes that gets the most regular use and where a family is most likely to interact. It is the place from which most people drive their daily lives. Its role, and often its physical location, is central to the home.

Kitchens also pose great design and construction challenges. To work efficiently, kitchens need to be able to accommodate multiple complex functions. They must allow for two or more people to work together, and even the occasional catering crew, but not feel vacant when used by only one. The concentration of storage, work surfaces, appliances, electronics, seating, and circulation calls for precise design, thoughtful organization, and careful coordination.

Due to cabinetry, refrigerators, stove hoods, and more, kitchens tend to need solid walls to enclose them. Yet for all the solidity required, contemporary lifestyles call for social connections from living spaces to kitchen, and thus a great degree of openness. Also, like all important spaces, they should have abundant natural light. They need to accommodate the chaos of cooking, but also facilitate social interaction when the inevitable happens and the party (or the family) gravitates to the spot where the lights are bright, there is a whirlwind of activity, and the smell of food makes the kitchen a convivial place to be.

Resolving the contradictions inherent in the functional needs takes some of the most intense design and construction work of the entire house. Kitchens can easily be the place in a home with the highest cost-per-square-foot, but for most families it is worth it. If the home is the country's spiritual center, at the heart of who we are as Americans, then the kitchen is the home's spiritual center, at the heart of the family.

Before our remaking of the kitchen at "Riptide" it was dark and without a view. Now it opens to a family room (see page 45, bottom left, and below) and dramatic harbor views.

Design and material options for kitchens are almost unlimited.

From cottage-style to contemporary and mostly open to other living space.

Displayed on this and the opposite page are six different kitchens in both new and renovated homes. All are well-lit and skillfully crafted to be both functional and beautiful.

The Primary Role of Eating Together: Dining Spaces

" … gastronomical perfection can be reached in these combinations: one person dining alone, usually upon a couch or a hill side; two people, of no matter what sex or age, dining in a good restaurant; six people, of no matter what sex or age, dining in a good home."

M.F.K. Fisher, *An Alphabet for Gourmets*, 1949

Facilitating eating together is a critical component of every home. The eating of meals is a basic human activity that binds families, and often families and friends, together. Frequently the dining space is directly adjacent to the entry hall. Sometimes other major circulation spaces within the house pass through the dining space, or at least adjacent to it and with views into it, in a reminder of the central role dining has in contented living.

In more casual, newer homes there are usually no traditional enclosed dining rooms, although they often remain in renovated historic homes. Space for formal dining on special occasions— and display of china, crystal, and silver— is only occasionally on the agenda. Casual homes usually have dining areas within a larger flowing space that encompasses kitchen, dining, and family gathering areas. The dining space is more informal this way, and also more flexible. It can be designed to feel right with a small table and fewer chairs, but to expand past its implied boundaries to accommodate a big group.

Informal dining is open to the kitchen, formal dining to the living room (page 54, bottom center).

Opposite: The dining space is central and partially open to living room, stair, and entry hall via a two-sided fireplace. The opposite view is shown on page 79, right.

Simple space at the "Moorings" impeccably restored and elegantly furnished.

A breakfast room with a grand fireplace and custom-made "boat hull" light trough.

Another central dining room in a formerly closed space now renovated to be open. The stair is separated within an aedicula. See page 61 for opposite view.

Dining amidst cherry display and great views.

A contemporary inglenook and a curved ceiling.

A river-rock fireplace. See page 40, bottom right.

Opposite: The space is gridded with panelling, windows, coffers, and, most of all, sunlight. See page 44, bottom left, for adjacent living space.

A Quiet Place to Think, Talk, or Work: Dens, Sunrooms, Studies

"To sleep well we do not need to sleep in a large room, and to work well we do not have to work in a den. But to dream of a poem, then write it, we need both."

Gaston Bachelard, *The Poetics of Space*, 1958

"Perchance the time will come when every house even will have not only its sleeping-rooms, and dining-room, and talking-room or parlor, but its thinking-room also … Let it be furnished and ornamented with whatever conduces to serious and creative thought."

Henry David Thoreau, *A Yankee in Canada*, 1853

Studies, sunrooms, or dens have largely replaced the formal living room in newer homes designed for casual living. Clients still need a quiet place off, or away from, the main living space, to interact with one or two others, to read, or to work. What they usually don't need is a place to entertain guests not welcome into the family space—a function the formal living room provides.

Studies, sunrooms, and dens are places to withdraw—to seek personal or shared refuge, to be inward focused, to let the imagination flow. Sometimes they become personal space for an individual, and there needs to be more than one separate personal space so each of a couple has their own. Paradoxically, today they may also be the place in the house most connected, via high-technology, to the outside world and to work. This is increasingly important in a wired world where work can be accomplished without face-to-face interaction, in a relaxed setting, without leaving home.

This sunroom is pulled off the northeast corner of the house and rotated to capture as much sun as possible but still have views to the north. Exterior, left and above (see page 28, top right; page 14; page 34, top right, and page 91). Interior, opposite (see page 89).

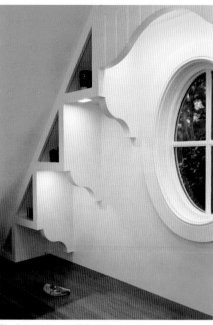

A cozy work space tucked under the roof. After living for several years in the house we designed for them (see page 27, top center), the client asked us back to create this room out of attic space.

Playful details, carefully integrated, in a place set up for work and contemplation.

Precise woodworking contributes to a sense of richness and repose in the study with fireplace shown to right.

Rugged stone contrasts with painted wood.

A cozy niche for when the grandkids visit.

The converted attic on the page opposite is adjacent to this study (above) and within the master suite. Woodwork creates a "roof" pattern above the fireplace and a hint of a pilaster at the bookshelves.

A two-story oak library, includes a traditional library stair.
Right: Walnut, painted wood, and cool repose.

Passage, Detail, Creating Surprise: Stairs & Circulation Spaces

By their nature, stairs have detail. They are complex assemblies of parts and they require precise design and great craftsmanship. They offer opportunities to establish character and create unexpected visual surprises. A banister, for example, can be both a banister and a flattened representation of an urn or a twisted rope.

The stair is usually the only vertical circulation in a house. It may be the only space that occupies a volume running from the lowest level to the highest. It requires a hole in the floor structure, and this can be enlarged so there is greater visual connection between the floor levels. Stairs and their adjacent openings let light, voices, and people pass up and down. A feeling of interior outlook can be provided at a stair opening's balcony edge, in contrast to feelings of shelter or coziness elsewhere in the house.

Stairs with intermediate landings are more comfortable to climb and are safer. Where space allows, they are preferable. The landing can be designed so it feels like a place for repose, in contrast to the treads and risers, which are a place for movement. Some stairs are like small rooms; others are like furniture inserted into a room, especially when risers, treads, banisters, hand rails, and wainscoting on adjacent walls work together to create an integral unit.

Circulation spaces should not be after-thoughts or left-over space. They play a critical role in the home as the organizers of other spaces and the zone of transition between them. They can do double-duty as galleries, libraries, or storage areas. They can be designed as rooms unto themselves, with character that results from shaped ceilings, well-designed details, and thoughtfully selected materials; or they can skirt the edge of another room, open to it or completely within it.

New stairs, circulation space, and floor openings transformed the existing interior of "Hydrangea Walk" from dark and dreary to light and open.

Opposite: A new aedicula with playfully inventive "Greek" columns opens the central core of "Riptide" (see page 54, top; page 10, right; and page 85, top left).

Three photos each of two dramatic stairs (this page and opposite) that evoke the fantastic and fun. Carpenters, glass artisans, masons, tile and carpet installers, and many others did their best work here. The 18th-century engraver, Piranesi, created images of complex imaginary spaces. These attempt to capture some of that character through the work of these highly skilled craftspeople.

Stair landing is a space unto itself with bench and niche.

Lovingly designed and executed stair parts with great variety, character, and precision.

Simple N.E. vernacular, crisp, bright, and dramatic.

Spiraling up to a finished attic loft space.

A niche and shaped ceiling at the top of the stair.

Above: Oak grandeur, detail, and an interior bay window.

Above and right: Different balustrades, dramatic spaces.

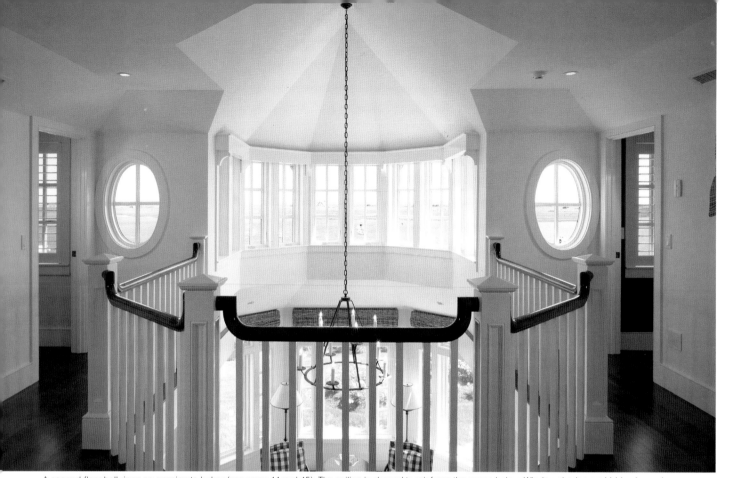

A second-floor hall rings an opening to below (see page 44 and 45). The ceiling is shaped to reinforce the space below. Window shades are hidden in a valence.

Casual front entry (left) and mud room entries (center and right) lead to circulation and living spaces beyond. Center photo shows a unique "picket fence" wainscot.

A "half-butterfly" plan configuration creates an embrace of the yard, landscape, and habor beyond. See page 93, exterior; 51 top, space to right; 47 bottom right, space to left.

Stair on page 65, top left, leads to hall with elegant, furniture-like details.

Small, highly charged, sculpted vestibule occurs off hall on page 42, top center.

Calm Retreat, Guest Rooms & Child's Play: Bedrooms

" … the bedroom is much more than just a place to sleep. It's a refuge within the refuge of the home—a snug nest from which we're meant to emerge restored and ready to face the larger domestic and outside worlds."

Winifred Gallagher, *House Thinking*, 2006

In contrast to living spaces, bedrooms are weighted toward private use. Their locations within the house must be based on balancing the need for privacy with the need for ready access to the rest of the house. Clients often want their master bedroom to have light and a view that is as good, or almost as good, as the family room. Often master bedrooms are placed on the first floor for ease of access. Sometimes when space, view, or other considerations cause them to be located on the second floor, an elevator (or a shaft for a future elevator) allows easy access.

In many cases bedrooms are fairly simple, being the place that is used the least when outdoor-focused, family-oriented living is primary. Others want bedroom suites that are quite elaborate, with work areas, sitting areas, his-and-hers dressing rooms, and more, within them. Simple or elaborate, master bedrooms often become a separate realm from the rest of the house. They allow an individual or a couple to retreat from their children or guests into a serene personal space.

A typical "signature" guest room at the Wequassett Resort overlooking Pleasant Bay.

A classical window looks out from the starry, starry night.

Built-in dressers and the underside of the roof shape define a cottage bedroom.

Opposite: The whole room projects into a bay window encompassing the panorama of marsh and ocean. See page 96, middle left, for exterior.

Above and opposite: Ten bedrooms with great variety, matching the variety in the people who occupy them and the beauty in their surroundings.

Water, Chrome, Glass, Fired Clay: Bathrooms

"Only place where no stress was felt,
And inner self curled up
To feel peace, was the bathroom."

Daniel Joseph, *Bathroom*, 2008

Bathrooms offer unique design and construction challenges because of the concentration and specificity of plumbing and waterproof materials and their fixtures. Like kitchens, they require a great deal of coordination, and skilled craftspeople to install them. They can vary greatly; from simple spaces off a mud room to clean up after being outside, to tiny but special powder rooms, to private or shared spaces for guests, to elaborate suites off the master bedroom.

Perhaps the master bath is the most secluded place of retreat in the home, and it is often subdivided even further to allow two people to use it at once with some privacy. It can be the most solitary place in the house and sometimes the most luxurious. It is a sanitary place for routine hygiene as well as a relaxing place for relieving stress. Moving water assists with both. A pleasurable, regenerating, spa-like setting is often the result.

Mirror reflection doubles this view-through space.

This new master bath is a bright and grand retreat. A cupola (see page 108, top right) brings light from above.

Above, left, and right: Two views of same space. Harbor is visible from tub, shower, and reflected in the mirror. See page 97, top right, for adjacent balcony shower.

Large glass tiles, sinks integral with linear vanity, and grass imbedded in interior window make a serene contemporary space.

A traditional shower with molded and mosaic tiles.

Variety and luxury in bathrooms, from contemporary, to classic, to Moroccan; from waves and dolphins cast into custom glass doors, to tiny oval glass tiles.

Seats, Fireplaces, Casework, Columns: Interior Details

Even the corner of a room can become a cozy spot to enjoy the view.

Treasures displayed on shelves defined by simple but playful pilasters.

"The fire confined to the fireplace was no doubt for man the first object of reverie, the symbol of repose, the invitation to repose … it gives a material form to man's festivities."

Gaston Bachelard, *The Psychoanalysis of Fire*, 1938

Interior details should make people want to touch them, to run their hands over the smooth billowing shapes of the moldings of a fireplace mantel or their fingers up and down the grooves and recesses of paneling or cabinet doors. This makes a home rich, interesting, and thought-provoking at the smallest of human scales.

Built-in casework, for storage behind doors or for open storage and display, can dramatically improve a home's efficiency and sense of order. It can also help a homeowner define who they are by the objects they display. Decorative columns as well, when they are special and designed to be appropriate for the individual house in which they are featured, can play a role in reinforcing the sense that the owner's home is uniquely theirs. Columns become signature details, pieces of invention, intended to provoke thought, wonder, and delight.

Window seats or inglenooks (built-in seats adjacent to a fireplace) provide low, cozy, intimate sub-spaces where one or two people can feel comfortable doing something different, apart from, yet still connected to, the main space. While a larger group plays a boisterous game of charades, for example, a more contemplative pair can look at a photo album together without feeling like they are snubbing the rest. Along with bay windows, these are much beloved spaces.

Fireplaces are very important, even when they do not get much use. The symbolic role the hearth plays in making a home feel warm, comfortable, and anchored to the ground, is ingrained in our psyches. The earliest dwellings in America—wigwams, tipis, and earth lodges—had central fires with openings above for exhaust. The earliest English colonial-era homes were planned around huge fireplace masses that allowed multiple fireplaces in different rooms to share the same whole-house warming chimney. Today, whether large or small, faced with rustic stone or formal moldings, fueled by wood or gas, fireplaces still provide focus, beauty, and warmth.

Seats for one (top), two (middle), or more.
Right: A rich and cozy space to enjoy nature.

The "Moorings" living room fireplace impeccably restored (see page 47, top right).

A two-sided fireplace is a pavilion of beautiful materials precisely integrated.

A crisp study fireplace in the library shown on page 59, bottom right.

A rustic fireplace flanked by narrow windows with tiny seats in niches.

The gallery space visible beyond (see page 41).

Another fireplace visible in library beyond.

Fireplace turns into a free-standing interior chimney pierced by an arched opening. An invented column is to the right.

Mantel was selected for its beautiful grain.

Simple paneling, tile, and pebbles in grout.

Carved stone mantel, stone piers, herringbone firebrick.

Elegant marble and elegant wood detailing.

Tile, bronze, and painted wood (see page 59, top right).

Stone cut to respond to "floating" mantel.

Precise woodwork (see page 78, top right).

Arts-and-crafts-inspired kitchen fireplace with herringbone brick pattern.

Right: Exaggerated details; elegant and fun.

Above and left: Two small, but rich, inglenooks.

A new surround for an existing fireplace.

Left: Cut stone "bricks" surrounded by classical detailing in wood.

Opposite: Variety in mantel detail, from classical to arts-and-crafts; in wood, brick, stone, and tile.

Above and two top center images: Three different shelf areas for display above cabinets for storage.

Above and below: symbolism in wood.

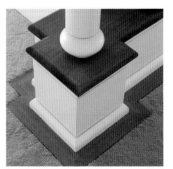

Above: A built-in buffet (left) and "his-and-hers" custom closet interiors (two bottom center images).

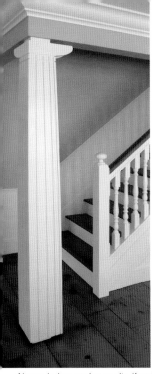

Above, below, and opposite (four images to the right): These wood columns were all custom-designed based on inventive ideas and crafted with care and precision.

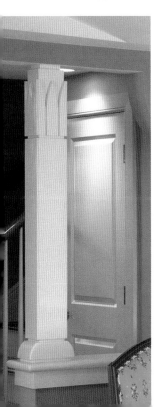

Defining Space, Scale & Character: Ceilings

Shaped ceilings can have dramatic effects on the spaces below. They can facilitate intimacy or define character through height, configuration, and detail. Coffers may add formality to a space while curved soffits may make it feel playful. Ceilings reinforce the sheltering nature of the roof and are sometimes the result of its slope. Spaces can soar vertically into high portions or tuck under low portions to compress into cozy shells for the occupant.

With open, flowing floor plans (where dining, kitchen, and family areas are visually connected), devices may be necessary to avoid the feeling of undifferentiated space. Shaped ceilings, along with columns, half-walls, and openings in walls, can imply separation while maintaining visual connection.

Ceiling height is important in making the scale of a space feel right, and it must be considered in relation to plan dimensions. A low ceiling may make a large space feel too spread out. A high ceiling may make a small space feel too tight.

Achieving variety in ceiling height is a challenge in locations with low height limits. Small changes, however, where relative rather than absolute heights are manipulated, can have a significant impact. An unusually low ceiling in an entry hall, for example, can make an average height in living spaces beyond feel taller. A low perimeter can make a slightly higher center feel taller as well. Patterns made by grids or paneling can give order to the space below and relieve the monotony of a flat, low ceiling or of large planes on a sloped ceiling.

Above and right: A three-story space crowned by a sloping ceiling that is pierced by triangular dormers and supported by broad arches and brackets. See page 41 & 63 for more of this space.

Ceiling curves up to create a ship's stern window. Asian-inspired balcony is beyond.

A hipped roof and dormer reflected in interior (see page 36, bottom right).

A Moorish arch playfully defines a tiny space just big enough for a child.

A bracket frames view to the space between wall and house (see page 23 & 114).

Fir boards on a three-dimensional "star"-shaped ceiling. A cupola pierces the center while pointed arches dance up and down the sides.

A traditional coffered ceiling with v-groove paneling with the grid.

A contemporary coffered ceiling and transom lights contrast with curved soffits.

Outlook, Repose, Connecting with Nature: Outdoor Living Spaces

"Beautiful landscape! I could look on thee
For hours,—unmindful of the storm and strife,
And mingled murmurs of tumultuous life."

William Lisle Bowles, *On a Beautiful Landscape*, 1789

There are great psychological, if not physical, rewards to a connection with the outdoors. People innately understand this and generally seek it in their homes. Peaceful communion with nature, even if it lasts just a few moments, can be an important, even inspiring, part of the day. A successful home facilitates this connection with nature.

Walking out onto balconies, decks, or terraces gives a feeling of connection to the world beyond. Balconies and decks that are well off the ground are dynamic vantage points for outlook while at the same time are protected because of the separation their elevation creates. Decks and terraces on or near the ground are reposeful places of rest or platforms for eating and socializing—places for outdoor living critical to casual houses in special landscapes.

Outdoor spaces should be zoned to feel like rooms, much like indoor spaces. They should be designed to be positive rather than left-over spaces; programmed for particular uses; located with regard to the breeze and the path of the sun; connected to other rooms, inside and out, in a deliberate sequence; and defined by actual or implied edges. Outdoor rooms may be created by architectural features (the walls of the house, decks, overhangs, porches, pools, stone walls, fences) or by natural features (planting beds, hedges, trees). Outdoor living space that is designed well, and in conjunction with interior space, helps connect a home and its occupants to the landscape. It helps create a world away from the worry and stress of everyday life.

Above and opposite: Contemporary gothicism in a woodland setting defines dynamic balcony, upper porch, and sunroom spaces (see page 56, 57 & 89, top).

Above and opposite: Porches, brackets, balconies, stairs, railings, and stone walls activate outdoor spaces and frame view.

Elegant and playfully stacked balconies for capturing view and breeze.

Opening from interior to exterior living spaces to harbor beyond.

Screened-in porch detailed to be both of the inside and the outside.

Stone path, well-selected plantings, terrace and a roof deck by the sea.

A winding bridge with a metal railing connects two raised terraces.

Multiple balconies, decks, and porches, transition inside to out.

Glass allows full view. Wequassett pool is beyond (see page 96, top right).

A classic white railing; brackets hold up a balcony above (see page 28, bottom right).

Pools and spas for play, relaxation, reflection, and exercise. The Wequassett Resort pool complex is top center and top right.

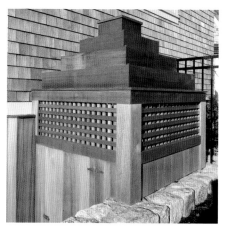

Outdoor showering is a special ritual and can have varying levels of privacy, whimsy, and light.

Garages, Guest Houses, Pavilions: Accessory Buildings

Beyond the basic function of providing automobile and other storage, a garage, especially when it is removed from the house, can become a back yard getaway; a place to be alone and to do things that might irritate others, like tinker with machines or blast rock & roll. The alternative rock band Deftones captured this purpose with the song *In the Garage*, their angst-ridden homage to "garage" bands. A guest house, as well, can provide freedom and privacy without giving up all connection to the family in the main house. Often the free-standing garage or guest house will appear to be a smaller, more casual version of the main house.

A pergola is an outdoor corridor, a path with three-dimensional definition. It directs passage through but can also, like a garage or guest house, define the edge of a space next to it, act as a screen between two spaces, or act as a screen between a space and something undesirable like a neighbor's driveway. An arbor is an outdoor doorway, celebrating entry and passage and highlighting a place to move through from one space to another. Both pergolas and arbors offer an architectural armature for roses or other climbing flowers. They allow a literal integration of architecture and nature. When covered with fully grown plantings, they create a special experience of nature—of being sheltered within plants rather than just gazing upon them.

When located in conjunction with outdoor dining space, outdoor kitchens can facilitate outdoor entertaining. Like all accessory buildings, however, placement on the site must be strategic and carefully coordinated to complement interior and exterior rooms. Otherwise, function is compromised and use is infrequent.

Stone walls border steps that lead to outdoor cooking and dining spaces.

A few years after pergola (opposite top) was built, roses had grown completely over top.

Above and opposite below: An invitation to joyful outdoor entertaining.

Above: Shingled piers, stone bases, and cedar structure on an arts-and-crafts pergola that defines the edge of the front yard and leads to the back yard.

Parking port for classic car behind classic village house.

A storage shed and outdoor bar next to a bocce court.

A small boat house at the edge of a salt marsh.

Entry portal to a bridge leading to an island.

Dining pavilion creates shadows and frames view.

Arbor abstracts pattern from door, page 42, top right.

Garage/guest house for house on page 35, bottom left.

Interior of outdoor kitchen (see page 98 & 99).

Above and opposite: Carriage house "Hydrangea Walk." Related but more casual than main house.

Adding & Extending Character: Before & After Transformations

"Not a log in this buildin' but its memories has got
And not a nail in this old floor but touches a tender spot …
But I tell you a thing right here, that I ain't ashamed to say,
There's precious things in this old house we never can
take away."

Will Carelton, *Out of the Old House*, *Nancy*, 1900

Additions and renovations pose distinct challenges. Designer and builder must be problem solvers committed to identifying and enhancing what is good, and fixing what is bad. It is rewarding when problems of circulation and function are solved, dark spaces are opened up to light, and ugly is made beautiful. Often transformations from before to after are dramatic. A bland house is given new character or a faded historic house is brought back to life. It may cost more to update historic houses than it does to replace them with simpler new houses, but the loss of the "precious things" embodied in the craft, details, and spatial quality of an antique is too great. Often additions to historic houses are "seamless," where existing character remains dominant and new and old are blended together without regard for telling them apart. Other times, distinct eras of growth are maintained and the new is visible as one more step in the evolution.

The interior spaces of the house are transformed through arches, ceiling shapes, detail, and light.

The existing was dull and low-quality.

Order, character, and playfulness were added to sound but bland and uninteresting existing houses

Above and middle: Transformed by bold new entry porches, brackets, dormers, gabels, windows, doors, shutters, and new materials.

Top left, middle left, and bottom left: Three dramatically different historic house fronts were enhanced by subtle and thoughtful additions and renovations.

Top right, middle right, and bottom right: The same three historic house fronts, shown to left, before being improved.

Top left, middle left, and bottom left: The same three historic house backs, shown to right, before being improved.

Top right, middle right, and bottom right: Three different house backs, opened up to light, view, and outdoor living.

Top left, middle left, and bottom left: The historic "Moorings" after being greatly improved by thoughtful additions and renovations, inside and out.

Top right, middle right, and bottom right: The "Moorings" before additions and renovations restored its former glory.

Top left, middle left, and bottom left: "House at Harding's General Store" before additions and renovations.

Top right, middle right, and bottom right: House at "Harding's General Store" after being transformed by additions and renovations, inside and out.

107

Top, middle, and bottom: "Hydrangea Walk," tired before new work.

Opposite and three images above: Historic front remains recognizable; the rest is all new.

Design Work in Process: Drawings & Models

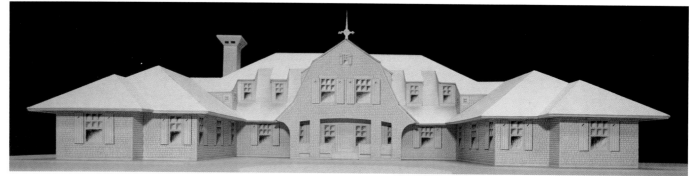

Wings project forward to create a three-sided entry court for a grand shingle-style house on a four-acre harborfront site.

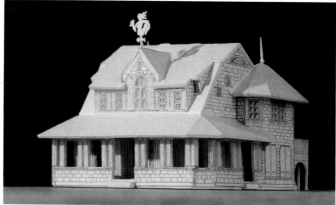

A compact, sculpted, and cheerful beach house on a flat site on Rhode Island's south coast. The mermaid brings flowers to the owner every day, all day.

Small scale guest house and barn on historic street create entry to large house beyond.

Front elevation from within the courtyard of house shown at left.

The site is long and narrow. This façade faces Mill Pond to the southeast.

Front elevation of charming new house. There will be great views from the tower.

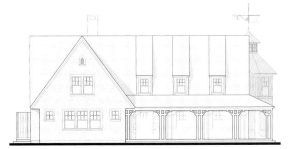

"Farm House" with Moroccan tile in the master bath (see page 71, bottom left).

Two sides of a grand house designed for a Cape Cod-like beachfront site in Holland.

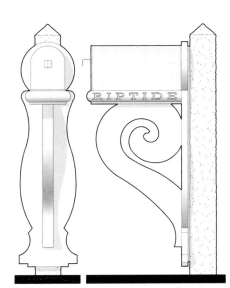

Perhaps the smallest project here—a mailbox for "Riptide" (see page 36 & 100, bottom left).

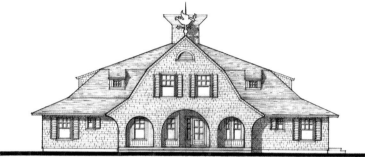

North (above) and east (right) elevations of a lakeside New England cottage. The screened-in porch and lake-facing façade are above left; entry façade is above right.

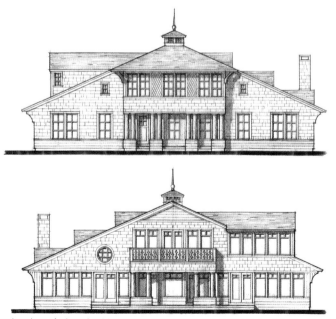

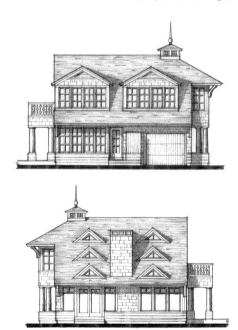

Four elevations of a broad-gabled shingle-style house. The design hints of McKim Mead & White's famous Low House in Bristol, Rhode Island.

Entry and screened porches added to an existing house.

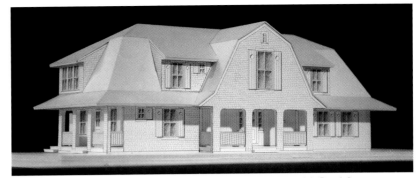

Front porch, side porch, and sculpted gambrel roof for a beach house at "Little Beach."

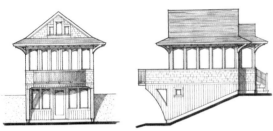

West (above), south (center), and east (right) elevations of the "Hen House," a 500-square-foot guest cottage.

A cottage designed for a village site.

Four elevations of a classic shingled "cottage" on a New England salt pond.

Directory of Projects and Photographs

Cape Cod Cove: Front dust jacket flap, 27 top center, 58 top left and top right, 59 top left and top right, 64 top center right and 80 bottom center by Dan Cutrona (DC); 10 left, 74 top left, 81 right, 85 bottom right, 96 bottom left and 114 by Brian Vanden Brink (BVB).

Cape Cod Farm: 75 bottom left and 114 by John DaSilva/ PSD (JD).

Cape Cod Museum of Art Exhibition, "Architecture of the Cape Cod Summer: The Work of Polhemus Savery DaSilva" (no index photo shown): 11 left and right by Randall Perry (RP).

Champlain's Bluff: 40 right, 42 top center, 47 bottom right, 51 top, 52 top, 54 bottom center, 59 bottom right, 67 top, 70 top center, 73 top right and left, 78 bottom left, 92 bottom left, 94 top right, 96 middle center, 97 top right, 114, and back cover by BVB; 67 bottom right, 93 and 96 bottom center by Paul Rochealu (PR); 67 bottom center and 100 top center by JD.

Cotchpinicut: 10 center, 15, 21 bottom left, 23, 24 top left, 28 top, 31 top, 34 top right, 36 top, 37 top left, 39, 41 left and right, 47 top left, 53, 56 left, 57, 63, 70 middle left, 74 middle left, 79, 83 left, 84 bottom left, 86, 87, 88 bottom left and right, 89 top, 90 and 91 by BVB; 14, 56 right, and114 by JD.

Dune House: Cover, 17 top, 19 top left, 24 bottom right, 30 top left, 35 bottom right, 70 top right, 84 top center left, and 114 by RP.

Fog Hollow: 64 top center left by DC; 114 by PR.
Fulling Mill, Martha's Vineyard (no index photo shown): Back dust jacket flap by JD.

Hallet's Hollow: 83 middle right, 89 bottom left, 102, 103 (except top), and 114 by RP. "Before" photos by PSD.

Harbor View: 18, 30 top right and bottom, 43 left and top and middle right, 58 bottom left and bottom right, 73 bottom right, 75 bottom right, 80 top right, and 84 top center right by DC; 34 bottom right, 43 bottom center, and 114 by JD; 43 bottom right by Gerry Madden/PSD (GM).

Harding's General Store: 98 top and bottom right, 99 bottom, 100 top left and bottom center, 107 top, middle, and bottom right by RP. "Before" photos by PSD.

Harding Shores: 70 bottom right and 114 by BVB.

Harper's Island: 89 bottom right, 92 top right, 100 top right and middle left, and 114 by BVB; 100 top right and middle left by JD.

Hydrangea Walk: 25, 32 bottom left, 38 top left, 72 right, 76 bottom, 77 middle left, 82 middle left and middle right, 92 top middle, 100 bottom right, 101, 108, 109, 114, and 116 by BVB; 52 bottom right, 60, 66 bottom right, and 68 bottom left by DC. "Before" photos on 108 by PSD.

Lake Wequaquet: 32 center, 50 top left, 83 top right, 95 top left, 97 bottom left, and 114 by DC. 19 bottom, 62 right, 66 bottom center, 77 right, and 85 top right by RP; 62 top and bottom left by PR.

Lower Cape: 20 top, 36 bottom right, 37 bottom left, 42 bottom right, 46 top, 54 bottom right, 70 bottom center, 74 bottom center, 84 top left, 85 bottom center left, 88 top right, and 114 by RP.

Marshview: 82 bottom left by JD; 114 by BVB.

The Moorings: 38 middle right, 42 top left, 47 top right, 52 bottom left, 70 middle center, 74 middle right, 78 top left, 106 top, middle, and bottom left, and 114 by BVB; 106 top, middle and bottom right by PSD.

Northgate Hill: 24 bottom center right, 85 bottom center right, and 114 by BVB.

Old Village House One (no index photo shown): 80 bottom left by RP.

Old Village House Two: 26 top right and 115 by RP.

Outer Cape: 82 top center and 115 by BVB.

Oyster Harbors: 27 top right, 51 bottom, 97 (middle row), 100 middle, 104 top left, 105 top right, and 115 by RP; 104 top right and 105 top left by PSD.

Oyster's Mermaid: 3, 9, 17 bottom, 19 top right, 26 top center, 29, 32 bottom right, 37 bottom right, 95 top right, and 115 by BVB; 38 middle left and 96 bottom right by JD; 26 top center and top right, 40 left, 65 right, 66 bottom left, 78 bottom right, 80 top left, and 97 (top left and top middle) by DC; 6 by RP.

Oyster River: 7, 13, 16 top, 21 top, 27 top left, 30 bottom, 33, 34 bottom left, 38 bottom right, 44, 45, 50 bottom right, 55, 64 bottom right, 66 top, 69, 74 middle center, 76 top, 82 top left, 96 middle left, and 115 by BVB.

Pepperwood: 65 top left, 67 bottom left, 75 bottom center, 78 top right, 94 bottom left, and 99 top by Peter Aaron/Esto (PA); 12, 37 top right, 64 top right, 81 top left, 84 bottom center right and left, 92 bottom right, and 115 by RP; 84 bottom right and 98 bottom left by JD.

Popponesset: 1, 4, 42 bottom center, 92 top left, back cover bottom left, and 115 by BVB.

Portside: 26 top left and bottom left, 34 top left and bottom center, 38 middle center, 64 top left and top center left, 73 bottom left, 75 top left and top right, 84 top center right, 97 bottom center, and 115 by DC; 97 bottom right by JD.

Quitnesset: 16 bottom left, 28 middle, 35 bottom left, 38 top center, 50 top right, 65 bottom left, 70 middle right, 74 top right, 77 top left and bottom left, 84 top center right, 89 top center right, 94 top left, 100 bottom left, and 115 by RP.

Riptide: 42 top right, 47 bottom left, 48, 49, 54 top, 61, 71, and 75 top center by BVB; 10 right, 38 bottom left, 84 top right, 85 top left, 100 middle right, 104 bottom, 105 bottom, and 115 by JD.

Sand Dollars: 59 bottom left, 70 top left, 74 bottom left, 82 bottom right, 85 bottom left, 88 top left, and 115 by BVB; 80 bottom right and 81 bottom left by JD.

Scattaree: 42 bottom left, 54 bottom left, 103 top right, and 115 by RP; 103 top left by PSD.

Sea Pine: 20 bottom left, 24 bottom center left, 50 bottom left, 74 top center, 82 middle center, and 115 by BVB; 28 bottom right, 38 bottom center, and 95 bottom right by DC.

Stage Neck: 20 bottom right, 24 top right, 46 bottom, 70 bottom left, 74 bottom right, 80 top center, 94 bottom right, 96 center right, and 115 by RP.

Sunset Lane: 68 bottom right, 83 bottom right, 104 middle left, 105 middle right, and 115 by RP; 104 middle right and 105 middle left by PSD.

Surfside, Nantucket: 82 bottom center and 115 by Greg Premru.

Wequassett Resort

Children's Center: 26 bottom right and 34 top left by JD; 27 bottom and 34 top right and top left by RP.

Pool Complex: 96 top left and top right by RP; 96 top center by Warren Jagger.

Pro Shop: 34 top center and 36 bottom left by RP.

Wequassett Resort

Signature Cottages: 16 bottom right, 21 bottom right, 24 bottom left, 38 top right, 64 bottom left, 68 top, 72 left, 82 top left, 92 bottom center, 95 bottom left, and 96 top right by RP.

Thoreau's Bar & Grill: 24 middle center by GM.

Final Words: by Clients, Critics, Writers, Awards Juries

"We feel the relaxation coming over us as soon as we get out of the car … and get a peek of the house through the trees. We love spending time here."

Harper's Island client quoted in *Better Homes and Gardens*

"Here is architecture sublimely contextual … teeming with exquisite details—rich and varied in their extreme beauty. One is constantly fascinated and at the same time always at ease when outside and inside these intriguing buildings. Viva the joy and wit, the elegance and charm, of this architecture which is ultimately mannerist in its complex and contradictory quality!"

Robert Venturi, architect and Pritzker Prize winner, from his foreword to *Architecture of the Cape Cod Summer*

"It was a joy both to read and to look at. I was particularly taken with the Harper's Island house, but I liked them all. I don't think anyone has done work that picks up on Venturi's themes and interprets them in as gentle, graceful, and understated a way as these houses do."

Paul Goldberger, architecture critic for *The New Yorker* upon reading *Architecture of the Cape Cod Summer*

"*Architecture of the Cape Cod Summer* makes a convincing case that the firm is achieving its goals … The overall high quality of the monograph … fully conveys what Venturi calls 'architecture sublimely contextual within the natural-rural, cultural-historical place that is Cape Cod.'"

Eve Kahn, reviewing *Architecture of the Cape Cod Summer* and quoting from Robert Venturi's foreword in *Period Homes*

"The work of Polhemus Savery DaSilva … takes on an individual route through the combination of contemporary and traditional design, paired with impeccable construction."

Rory Marcus, Cape Cod Museum of Art

"Playfulness is seen … from every vantage point, both interior and exterior. The house is an artful reinterpretation of a classic lakeside retreat, a place where time is suspended, and where rich family comforts, traditions, and memories abound. It is a house intended to liberate its inhabitants from worldly cares … and to restore a child's sense of play, wonder, and possibility."

Terry Ward Libby, on House on Lake Wequaquet in *Cape Cod Magazine*

"New additions and alterations sensitively convey the character of the original design, yet provide all the amenities of modern life."

Bulfinch Awards Jury on the Moorings

" … an example of great attention to detail resulting in a very interesting, and livable, home."

Richard Wright, on Pepperwood in *Hearth & Home*

"[They] are architectural history enthusiasts. They troll ancient building cultures knowing … that layering visual allusions to remoter realms enrich experience and make buildings memorable."

Ellen Weiss, architectural historian, in *Cape Cod Magazine*

"A whimsical design that references traditional elements in a light-hearted manner."

Bulfinch Awards Jury on Wequassett Pro Shop

"The longer I live in the house the more I understand the care and creativity that went into the design and construction. I see how the house works with the sun as it moves through the day. I see how every detail was intentional and carefully crafted. I am still surprised by the odd bit of whimsy. The house feels right to me, and special too. It is elegant while being casual and practical. It is unique but not out of place. It doesn't look quite like any other house I have seen, yet it is comfortable on our site and in our neighborhood. It was a joy to build it, and it is a joy to live in it."

House on Lower Cape client